REALLY ROTTEN JOKES

1st spider — "I'm famous now!"
2nd spider — "Why do you say that?"
1st spider — "Didn't you see me on the television last night?"

Bill — "I tried to swat a fly that was crawling on the television last night!"
Will — "Did you hit it?"
Bill — "No — but I got it on video!"

What do chickens eat on special occasions?

Layer cake!

Waiter — "Would you like to try some of our bullet salad sir?"
Diner — "I've never heard of such a thing before. Why do you call it that?"
Waiter — "Because there are slugs in it, sir."

Diner — "Waiter! There are two flies splashing about in my coffee!"
Waiter — "Not splashing about, sir — they're swimming for the cup!"

Diner — "Waiter! My teeth are stuck in a bit of steak!"
Waiter — "Don't you mean a bit of steak has got stuck in your teeth?"
Diner — "No — my false teeth stuck in the steak — look, there they are on the plate, beside the lettuce!"

Diner — "Waiter, bring me a plate of spaghetti, and step on it!"
Waiter — "Oh, no, sir, I'll spoil my new shoes!"

Diner — "Do you play tennis?"
Waiter — "Yes, sir!"
Diner — "Then get some coaching on your service — it's rotten!"

Diner — "I'll have the steak pie, please!"
Waiter — "Anything else?"
Diner — "A hammer and chisel to eat it with!"

Diner — "Look out of the window! See how the sun is slowly sinking and the hills are tipped with gold!"
Waiter — "At times like this, sir, I wish I was a hill!"

Diner — "Waiter! There's a tooth in my cream!"
Waiter — "There's a dentist at the next table — I'll ask him to whip it out!"

Diner — "You've brought me a glass full of muddy brown liquid — I asked for still water!"
Waiter — "It may be muddy and brown, but I can assure you, it's still water, sir!"

Waiter — "What? MORE salt and pepper, sir?"
Diner — "Yes, please — they're the only things that are keeping me from starving in this place!"

1st Waiter — "I hate New Year's Eve!"
2nd Waiter — "I know — all those tablecoths to change!"

Diner — "I'll have the fish — no, make it a steak!"
Waiter — "I'm not a magician, sir!"

Diner — "May I use your telephone, please?"
Waiter — "Is it urgent?"
Diner — "I'll say it is — I'm calling the Missing Portions Bureau!"

Diner — "I asked for a game bird, but this is just chicken!"
Waiter — "But that chicken's a game bird too, sir — it was playing snakes and ladders when it died!"

An astronaut walks into Al the butcher's shop.
Al — "What are you doing here?"
Astronaut — "N.A.S.S.A.!"
Al — "So you're from space headquarters!"
Astronaut — "No — Need Another String of Sausages, Al!"

Joiner — "That's the job done, sir!"
Chess player — "Great! Will you take a check, mate?"

Two robots are sitting on a park bench, munching on a couple of cans of beans.

1st robot — "Crust's nice and crunchy!"
2nd robot — "Yes, but I don't think much of the filling!"

1st Diner — "I'll have the steak and chips, and a glass of water, please!"

2nd Diner — "I'll have the same — and make sure my glass is clean!"

Later . . .

Waiter — "Here is your order, gentlemen
. . . now, which one of you wanted the clean glass?"

Waiter — "Can I take your order, sir?"

Diner — "Certainly not! I'm paying for it, and I'm eating it!"

Diner — "Why is my cake soaking wet?"

Waiter — "It's a bath bun!"

Waiter — "I'm sorry, sir, but there's nothing left in the kitchens!"

Diner — "But you're carrying a trayful of food — what do you call that?"

Waiter — "My dinner!"

French Diner — "The dishes we have
in France are far superior to your English ones!"

Waiter — "Why? Are they unbreakable!"

Diner — "You say the ham is home-cured?"

Waiter — "Yes, sir!"

Diner — "Well, the cure didn't work —
it still doesn't look at all well!"

Diner — "Can I have a doggy bag, please?"

Waiter — "Certainly, sir!"

Diner's son — "Gosh, Dad — have we got a dog?"

Mum — "How's school?"
Son — "On the up!"
Mum — "On the up?"
Son — "Yes — sit up, stand up, own up, speak up and shut up!"

Fred — "There was a fire in the cobblers' premises today, and the cobblers sent up an S.O.S."
Ted — "What does S.O.S. stand for?"
Fred — "Save Our Soles!"

What is the difference between a married man and a single man?
One kisses the missus and the other misses the kisses!

Diner — "I've been waiting here for half-an hour! It's disgraceful!"
Waiter — "I've been waiting here for seven years, and you don't hear me complaining!"

Diner — "Do you do fast-food here?"
Waiter — "Well, we have a nice rocket salad on the menu!"

Diner — "Waiter! There are no currants in this currant bun!"
Waiter — "So what? There are no angels in the angel cake!"

Diner — "Waiter! There's no beef in my beefburger!"
Waiter — "Correct, sir — and there's no horse in your horseradish!"

Diner — "Waiter! I have a complaint!"
Waiter — "In that case, sir, you'll have to leave — it might be infectious and we're very strict about health regulations here!"

Diner — "Last time I ate here, the steak made me sick for a week!"
Waiter — "Please don't bring that up again, sir!"

Diner — "Why is that dog staring at me like that?"
Waiter — "I don't know sir — perhaps he doesn't like you using his plate!"

Diner — "I'm afraid that once I've paid this bill, I'll have no money left for a tip for you!"
Waiter — "Hang on, sir, and I'll see if I can take something off the total!"

Diner — "I see the portions are getting more generous at last!"
Waiter — "How can you tell, sir?"
Diner — "Yesterday, there was a fly paddling in my soup. Today, it's having to swim!"

Waiter — "Do you like tagliatelli, sir?"
Diner — "I haven't come here to discuss opera. I want something to eat!

Diner — "I'm so hungry I could eat a horse!"
Waiter — "Sorry sir, horse is off tonight!"

Waiter — So you're an actor, sir?
Then perhaps you'd like a Shakespearean steak!"
Diner — "Shakespearean steak? What's that?"
Waiter — "It's cooked 'As You Like It', sir!"

Why is a waiter like an athlete?
Because he runs for cups and plates!

Diner — "Come here, young man — I've a tip for you!"
Waiter — "Sir?"
Diner — "Yes, here it is — don't bring your girlfriend here — the food's terrible and the service is worse!"

Headless ghost — "I'm so hungry, my stomach think's my throat's been cut!"
Waiter — "I-I-I h-h-hate to tell you this, sir, b-b-ut it has!"

Waiter — "One pound for a cup of coffee, sir and the refills are free!"
Diner — "I'll just have a refill, then!"

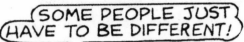

Diner — "Waiter! The water in my glass is cloudy!"
Waiter — "Don't worry sir — the water's perfectly fine. It's just a dirty glass, that's all!

Waiter — "Would you like to try some of our special two-handed cheese, sir?"
Diner — "Two-handed cheese?"
Waiter — "Yes — hold the cheese with one hand and your nose with the other!"

Waiter — "Just one egg, sir?"
French Diner — "Yes, please. One egg is un oeuf!"

Diner — "Waiter! There's a splinter of wood in my ice cream!"
Waiter — "That pesky fly must have left its snowboard behind, sir!"

Waiter — "Before you order, sir, I should tell you that the steak's off, the fish is off, the vegetarian dish is off and the chef's off!"
Diner — "I'm off as well, then!"
Diner — "Is that onion soup I smell?"
Waiter — "It is and you do, sir."

Diner — "I'll have the ploughman's lunch, please!"
Waiter — "Sorry, sir, but the ploughman got here before you!"

A boy is watching in admiration as a waiter comes out of the kitchen, carrying four plates on each arm and whistling.

"That's very clever! How do you manage to do it?" he says.
The Waiter replies — "Easily! I just pucker up my lips and blow!"

Diner — "I'd like four scoops of ice cream, two slices of apple pie, a piece of chocolate cake and lots of whipped cream!"
Waiter — "And a cherry on top?"
Diner — "Oh, no! I'm watching my weight!"

Diner — "Waiter! This egg is bad!"
Waiter — "Don't blame me, sir, I only laid the table!"

Waiter — "Is there a problem with your food, sir?"
Diner — "The food looks delicious, but I'm afraid I can't eat it!"
Waiter — "Why is that sir?"
Diner — "Because you haven't brought me a knife and fork!"

Diner — "Waiter! There's a worm on my plate!"
Waiter — "That's not a worm, sir, that's your sausage!"

Diner — "I'll have the chef's salad, please!"
Waiter — "That's hardly fair, sir — chef hasn't had a thing to eat since breakfast time!"

Waiter — "Enjoying your coffee, sir?"
Diner — "No! It tastes just like mud!"
Waiter — "Well, sir, it was fresh ground this morning!"

Diner — "Just look at the state of your shirt! It's covered in jelly and custard!"
Waiter — "Yes, sir, one does get a trifle messy in this line of work!"

Diner — "Waiter! There's a cockroach in my soup!"
Waiter — "Don't worry, sir. There isn't enough in your plate to drown him!"

Diner — "Waiter, can you describe to me exactly what it is that I have just eaten?"

Waiter — "Why, sir?"
Diner — "They'll want to know when I reach hospital!"

Diner — "Waiter! Do you have frog's legs?"
Waiter — "Yes, sir!"
Diner — "Well, hop off to the kitchen to get my order, then!"

Diner — "Waiter! There's a caterpillar in this lettuce! What have you got to say about it?"
Waiter — "Well, it's green, hairy, about an inch long ..."

Waiter — "You haven't touched your custard, sir — is there a problem?"
Diner — "I'll say there is! It's so rubbery that there's a fly on it using it as a trampoline!"

Diner — "Waiter! I've bitten my tongue!"
Waiter — "And did it taste any better than the steak, sir?"

Waiter — "I don't see why you're complaining, sir. There's nothing wrong with your food."
Diner — "Nothing wrong with it? Even the flies are turning away from my plate!"

Diner — "Waiter, I can't eat this! The steak is too tough, the fries are burnt to a crisp and the peas are as hard as marbles! Have you got anything that's a little easier to swallow?
Waiter — "How about a glass of water, sir?"

Diner — "Waiter! There's a dead insect in this bottle of wine!"
Waiter — "Well, sir, you did ask for something with a little body in it!"

Jim — "I've just had dinner at that new restaurant in town."
Joe — "What was it like?"
Jim — "The food was fine, but the bill was a bit hard to swallow!"

Diner — "Waiter! There's a bluebottle in my stew!"
Waiter — "Yes, sir, it's the rotten meat that attracts them!"

Diner — "Waiter! There's a flea in my custard!
Waiter — "Just tell him to hop it, sir!"

Diner — "What's today's special?"
Waiter — "Yesterday's leftovers, sir!"

Diner — "Waiter! There's a fly in my starter!"
Waiter — "Hold on, sir, and I'll ask him if he's ready for your main course yet!"

Diner — "Waiter! There are TWO flies in my soup!"
Waiter — "Yes, sir. I'm afraid neither of them liked the look of what your friend was having!"

Diner — "Waiter! What's this spider doing in my alphabet soup?"
Waiter — "Looks like he's trying to spell 'help', sir!"

Waiter — "What's the matter, sir — curry a little too spicy?"
Diner (Sarcastically) — "Naw! I always have smoke coming out of my ears!"

Diner — "Waiter! There's a slug in my salad! I can't eat it"
Waiter — "Why not, sir? Are you a vegetarian?"

Bill — "I couldn't get what I wanted at the fry bar!"
Will — "What was that?"
Bill — "Chocolate chips!"

Prison visitor — "I hear you let the prisoners borrow classical CD's from the prison library."
Prison governor — " Yes, but only one Purcell."

What kind of music can you play on a lemonade bottle?
Pop!

Notice on music shop's door "Gone for lunch. Bach in fifteen minuets."

Many years ago, a man went to see his old friend, who was a composer. He knocked on the door, but there was no answer. "Come on out," he shouted. "I know you're Haydn in there somewhere!"

What musical instrument do lumberjacks play?
The TIMBER!-ine!

What did the fat musician write on his refrigerator door?
"Sibelius too round — Schumann!"

Little boy (home from music lesson) — "I played Bach today!"
Mum — "That's nice dear — did you win?"

"I used to play the drums when I lived in the Outback in Australia — then I stopped beating around the bush!"

What kind of music do blacksmiths like?
Heavy metal!

Who are the most untrustworthy members of the orchestra?
The fiddlers!

Do musicians give each other presents on their birthdays?
No — they just exchange chords!

How did the musician get locked out?
Because he'd got the wrong key!

What musical instrument did they play in Ancient Britain?
The Anglo-saxophone!

What musical instrument to fishermen play?
The cast-a-net!

"I used to play the triangle, but now I want to do some ting else."

"I used to play the piano, but now I'm having a bash at the drums."

"I used to play the bagpipes, but I became disenchantered."

"I used to play the trombone, but my playing began to slide."

"My brother plays the harp — he's a plucky little fellow!"

What kind of music do ghosts like?
Boo-gie woo-gie!

"My sister's just smashed her violin to smithereens!"
"What did she say when she did it?"
"Fiddlesticks!"

"What's that rabbit doing on your violin?"
"That's not a rabbit — that's my hare on a G string!"

"I used to play percussion, but I couldn't drum up any enthusiasm for it."

"Did you ever own a musical instrument?"
"Well, I used to have some drumsticks. . .
— but I cooked them and ate them!"

What do you call five boulders with guitars?
A rock band!

"Are you nervous about your singing solo tonight, Madame Bellows?"
"Nervous? I'm up to high doh!"

Q What kind of music do woodcutters listen to when they're relaxing?
A Chopin.

Notice on musician's front door:
"Handel not working. Please use Bach door."

Visitor to musician's house — "What's this on your fridge? (reads) 'Peas, piano, bread, violins. . . '
Musician — "That's my Chopin Liszt!"

Teacher — "For your geography lesson today, I want you to draw me a map of the school!"
Pupil — "Don't you know your way around yet?"

Pupil — "Miss! Miss! Joey's swallowed a bottle of ink!"
Teacher — "Incredible!"
Joey — "No — indelible!"

Teacher — "What comes after 'O'?"
Pupil — "Yeah!"
Teacher — "name four animals from the cat family!"
Pupil — "Mummy Cat, Daddy Cat and two kittens!"

Teacher — Name the Scottish engineer who invented a steam engine.
Pupil — What, sir?
Teacher — Well done! Watt!

Teacher — "The principal, Mr Smith is going to be retiring at the end of this year, children!"
Pupil — "So he decided to quit while he was a head, did he!"

Teacher — "Are you chewing gum?"
Pupil — "No miss — I'm Billy Smith!"

Teacher — "Well done, Watkins. You're in good time for the English essay exam but what's that bit of wood for?
Watkins — "Well, sir, that's my writer's block!"

Teacher — "What is the least used bone in your body?"
Pupil — "My head!"

Teacher (in chemistry class) — "Whatever is the matter, Simpkins? You're trembling all over!
Pupil — "I'm following the instructions for this experiment, sir. It says 'Add liquid to test tube, then shake for two minutes!'"

Teacher — "Can anyone give me an example of something you take for granted, but which didn't exist 200 years ago?"
Pupil — "My mum!"

Teacher — "What does 'N-E-W' spell?
Pupil — "New!"
Teacher — "and if we add a 'K'?"
Pupil — "Canoe!"

Billy — "Our teacher's like a bird of prey — she's eagle-eyed and watches us like a hawk!"

Teacher — "Annie, you're pretty dirty, aren't you?"
Annie — "Yes — and I'm even prettier when I'm clean!"

Teacher — "Why are you late, George?"
George — "I had to say goodbye to my pets!"
Teacher — "It doesn't take long to say goodbye to a couple of rabbits or a dog!"
George — "No — but I've got an ant farm!"

Teacher — "What is a fortification?"
Pupil — "Two times a twentyfication!"

Teacher — "Can anyone name a deadly poison?"
Pupil — "Aviation — one drop and you're dead!"

Teacher — "What have you got in your pockets, Smithers?"
Smithers — "Holes!"

Teacher — "Which month has twenty-eight days?"
Pupil — "All of them — and some have a few extras!"

Teacher — "Who's that girl walking across the playground? She looks like Helen Brown!"
Pupil — "She doesn't look much better in red, Miss!"

Pupil — "I'm glad I wasn't born in Spain, Miss!"
Teacher — "Why is that, Jimmy?"
Pupil — "because I can't speak Spanish!"

Teacher — "What family does the whale belong to?"
Pupil — "Can't be any family round here, miss — no-one's got a bath big enough to keep one!"

Teacher — "And now Annie's going to play something for us on her violin. Are you going to play by ear, Annie?"
Annie — "No — I'm going to play over there!"

Teacher — "If b = 10, a = b + 6 and c = b - a, what is c?
Pupil — "It's a whole lot of salty water surrounded by beaches, sir!"

Teacher — "Can you give me two examples of pronouns, Jimmy?"
Jimmy — "Who, me?"
Teacher — "Correct!"

Teacher — "Can anyone give me a sentence starting with 'I'?"
Pupil — "I is — "
Teacher — "I am, I AM!"
Pupil — "I AM the ninth letter of the alphabet!"

Teacher — "Mrs Jones, your son has a perfect attendance record, so I've decided to give him a week off school!"
Mrs Jones (proudly) — "Ah, so he deserves a break!"
Teacher — "No, Mrs Jones — I do!"

Teacher — "How are you enjoying your singing lessons, Ray?"
Pupil — "Me? Ray? Hum . . . soh-fah, so good!"

Teacher — "What do John F. Kennedy, Abraham Lincoln and George Washington have in common?"
Pupil — "Well, sir, they're all people I have never heard of!"

Teacher — "What are two two's?"
Pupil — "Frilly dresses for ballet dancers, miss!"

Teacher — "Derek, do you think you're the person in charge of this class?"
Derek — "No, miss."
Teacher — "Then stop acting the goat!"

Teacher — "You have all heard of the Ice Age, and the Stone Age — what age do you live in today?"
Annie — "My mum says I'm at a difficult age!"

Teacher — "What is a quart?"
Pupil — "A place where a judge works!"

Teacher — "What did Charles II do when he came to the throne?"
Pupil — "He sat down!"

Pupil (to friend) — "What will I do? I can't see the blackboard!"
Friend — "Don't worry — there's nothing interesting on it at the moment!"

Teacher — "Can anybody tell me where Cleopatra's needle is?"
Pupil — "In her sewing box!"

Teacher — **"What is one twentieth of a half?"**
Pupil — **"Not big enough to bother about!"**

Teacher — "Why did you fail your maths exam, Billy? You did so well last time!"
Pupil — "This time my mother washed my shirt and the answers came off my cuff!"

Teacher — "Why aren't you facing the front, like the rest of the class, Jimmy?"
Jimmy — "Because you said you'd be glad to see the back of me!"

Teacher — **"I'm sorry, Mrs Smith, but your son is way behind in his maths lessons!"**
Mrs Smith — **"But he told me that he sat at the front of the class!"**

Teacher — "You got all your maths homework wrong last night, Annie. I can't understand it!"
Annie — "Neither could I!"

Teacher — "If I took a cake and sliced it in four, and then cut each quarter into ten pieces, what would I have?"
Pupil — "Crumbs!"

Teacher — "Why do you want to become an astronaut, Bobby?"
Bobby — "Because I can't think what on earth to do when I grow up!"

Teacher — "Can anyone give me a sentence using the word 'centimetre'?"
Pupil — "My grandma got the train up from London, and my Dad was centimetre at the station!"

Teacher — "Jimmy — can you spell the other word for bucket? Is it p-a-i-l with an i or p-a-l-e with an e?
Jimmy — "No idea!"
Teacher — "Wrong! — And don't call me dear!"

Teacher — "Why are you biting your pencil, Annie?"
Annie — "I can't find my sharpener!"

Teacher — "What makes you think that Adam and Eve lived on cheese?"
Pupil — "You told us they lived in the Garden of Edam!"

Teacher — "Mrs Brown, I'm afraid your son's rather wet!"
Mrs Brown — "That's a terrible thing for a teacher to say about any pupil!"
Teacher — "But it's true! — He fell in the school swimming pool five minutes ago!"

What is the penalty for bigamy?
Two sets of in-laws!

1st sailor — "The barometer's falling!"
2nd sailor — "Rotten weather ahead?"
1st sailor — "No — rotten nail that was holding it on the wall!"

Why did the bus go mad?
It was driven to distraction!

Mother — "If you found a five-pound note on the street, would you keep it?"
Billy — "Of course not!"
Mother — "What a good boy! What would you do with it?"
Billy — "I'd spend it!"

Teacher — "Now, children, you should never be afraid to ask questions. Asking questions helps you get along!"
Billy — "In that case, can I get along home now?"

Teacher — "Now, children, I want you all to be very quiet, for I'm not feeling very well today!"
Johnny — "You should do what my mum does when she's not feeling very well, miss!"
Teacher — "And what does your mummy do, Johnny?"
Johnny — "She sends us outside to play!"

Teacher — "Do you know your grammar, Sadie?"
Sadie — "Of course I do — she lives with my gramper just along the road from us!"

Teacher — "I'm afraid your behaviour goes against the spirit of this school, Billy!"
Billy — "Aren't you too old to believe in ghosts, miss?"

Teacher — "Can anyone tell me anything about the Arctic Circle?"
Pupil — "It's like my dad's head — a great white bare place!"

Teacher — "Who invented fractions?"
Pupil — "Henry the eighth, Miss!"

Teacher — "Can anyone give me a sentence using the word 'coincide'?"
Pupil — "If it starts raining during the lunch break the headmaster tells us to coincide."

Betty — "I've just come from the beauty salon!"
Barbara — "What a pity it was shut!"

Old gentleman — "And what does your father do, sonny?"
Little boy — "He drives other people's cars!"
Old gentleman — "So he's a chauffeur, is he?"
Little boy — "No — he's a car thief!"

Mother — "Jimmy, do you think your little brother can tell me what nationality was Napoleon?"
Jimmy — "Corsican!"

Notice outside head teacher's office — "There is no such thing as a free education. All pupils must pay attention or pay the penalty!"

Molly — "How can I make a sculpture of myself out of this bit of clay?"
Mo — "Easy! Just take away all the bits that don't look like you!"

Teacher — "What's wrong with Joe, Tom?"

Tom — "He's bashful, that's all."

Teacher — "Bashful?"

Tom — "Yes, Miss. We were fighting at playtime, and now he's bash-full!"

Teacher — "You were sick and missed school yesterday, didn't you, Billy?"

Billy — "Yes and No, sir."

Teacher — "What do you mean — yes and no?"

Billy — "Yes, I was sick. No, I didn't miss school one little bit!"

Teacher — "Can anyone tell me the name of the first woman on earth?"

SILENCE

Teacher — "Come along children, someone must know — think of an apple!"

Billy — "Granny Smith!"

Teacher — "Now, children, in this picture you will see a kangaroo. A kangaroo is a native of Australia. . . What's the matter, Freddy?"

Freddy — "My auntie's married to one of those!"

Teacher — "Can anyone tell me what the word 'adult' means?"

Pupil — "An adult is a person who has stopped growing at both ends and has started growing round the middle!"

Teacher — "Why are you the only one in class today, Katie?"

Katie — "Because I'm the only one who didn't eat school dinner yesterday!"

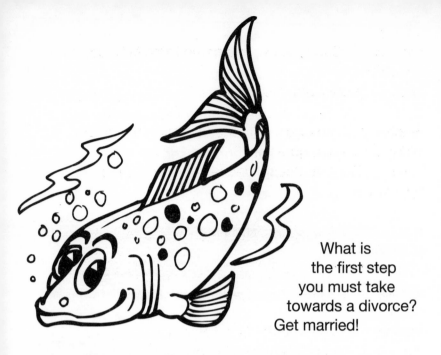

What is
the first step
you must take
towards a divorce?
Get married!

What did one plank say to the other one?
Are you coming to the board meeting?

Woman in dress-shop — "Can I try on that pink dress in the window?"
Assistant — "Oh, no, ma'am, you'll have to use the changing-rooms!"

The politician finished addressing the crowd outside the shopping centre, but before he stepped down, he asked if there were any questions.
"Yes," said a small boy in the front of the crowd, "can I have the box you're standing on when you've finished with it?"

What can catch runaway burglars from ten feet away?
The long arm of the law!

Teacher — "Can anyone here name three famous Poles?"
Pupil — "North, South and tad, sir!"

Teacher — "The exam will take one hour; that's ten minutes for each question."
Pupil — "But that doesn't leave any time for the answers!"

Teacher — "Why haven't you done your Geography homework?"
Pupil — "My Dad says the world is changing, so I decided to wait until it was finished."

Teacher — "What are the Great Plains?"
Pupil — "Concorde, and the jumbo jets!"

Teacher — "Where is Hadrian's Wall?"
Pupil — "Round Hadrian's garden, sir!"

Teacher — "When was Rome built?"
Jimmy — "At night, sir!"
Teacher — "Why do you say that?"
Jimmy — "Because my mother's always saying that Rome wasn't built in a day!"

Teacher — "What do you know about the Dead Sea, Annie?"
Annie — "Not much, Miss — I didn't even know it had been ill!"

Teacher — "Who discovered the atom?"
Pupil — "Eve!"

What do you say when you hear a ghost on the other side of your bedroom wall?
"Just come on through!"

"Guard! Guard! The carriage is on fire!"
"That's all right sir — it's a smoking carriage!"

Golfer (to caddie) "What should I take for my next shot?"
Caddie — "Golf lessons!"

What was the name of the legendary Spanish detective?
El C.I.D!

Teacher — "Billy! I'm not going to tell you to stop talking again!"
Billy — "Thank goodness for that! I can't think what I'm saying with all these interruptions!"

Teacher — "Harry, please don't whistle while you're working."
Harry — "It's all right, Miss, I'm not working, just whistling!"

Teacher — "Is there any wildlife in the Amazonian jungle?"
Pupil — "The parrots can get quite angry, sir!"

Teacher — "What is an island, Jimmy?"
Jimmy — "It's a bit of land, surrounded by water, except on one side!"
Teacher — "Except on one side?"
Jimmy — "Yes, sir — the top!"

Teacher — "What's the matter, Joe?"
Joe — "When I try to do maths, I feel like a ship!"
Teacher — "What do you mean?"
Joe — "I'm all at sea!"

Teacher — "Can anyone give me a sentence using the word 'defence'?"
Pupil — "Our dog keeps escaping from the back garden, so Dad's going to mend defence!"

Teacher — "Where is the English Channel?"
Pupil — Press the right button on your TV remote and you'll find it, sir!"

A king of a far-off country went out and bought a bottle of perfume and a bottle of poison. The perfume was for his future queen and the poison was for his deadliest enemy. He wrapped them up and put the same note in with each parcel — "A little drop of something to sweep you off your feet ..."

Teacher — "Is there any wildlife in the Arctic?"
Pupil — "No, Miss, it's too cold for parties!"

Teacher — "What do we do with crude oil?"
Billy — "We could teach it some manners, sir!"

Teacher — "How do we know that the world is round?"
Pupil — "Because my mum and dad say it is!"

Teacher — "What's five times five?"
Annie — "That's the third time you've asked us that, Miss. Can't you remember the answer?"

Teacher — "Can anyone tell me anything about Robinson Crusoe?"
Billy — "Yes, miss — he lived on a desert island and turned red!"
Teacher — "Turned red?"
Billy — "Yes — it said in my book that he was marooned!"

Teacher — "Why didn't you do your homework, Billy?"
Billy — "You were looking so, tired, Miss, that I didn't want to give you any more problems!"

Teacher — "If you multiplied 15 by 20 and divided the answer by 5, what would you get?"
Pupil — "The wrong answer, probably, sir!"

Teacher — "If I had five oranges in one hand and six in the other, what would I have?"
Pupil — "Very big hands!"

Walt — "So how was the food on the channel crossing?"
Ike — "It went down quickly — but it came up really fast!"

Bill — "You remind me of Lord Neilson!"
Will — "Don't you mean Lord Nelson?"
Bill — "No — you remind me of Neilson — before he lost his i!"

Did you hear about the geologist who married a gardener?
They built a rock garden together!

"This is a picture of Benjamin Franklin!"
"You're kidding me — he's not franklin' — he's just standin' there!"

Teacher — "If you had five pounds and you asked your father for another two, how many pounds would you have?"
Pupil — "Five, sir!"
Teacher — "You don't know your arithmetic, my lad!"
Pupil — "You don't know my father, sir!"

Teacher — "What time do you wake up in the morning, Johnny?"
Johnny — "About two hours after I get to school, Miss!"

Pupil — "Can you send my exam results to my parents by e-mail, please, miss?"
Teacher — "But you don't have a computer at home, Jimmy!"
Pupil — "That's right, miss!"

Teacher — "What is half of eight?"
Pupil — "Sideways, it's three, and up and down it's zero!"

Teacher — "How are you getting on with the novel I asked you to read, Jimmy?"
Jimmy — "I got stuck at page ten, miss."
Teacher — "How is that?"
Jimmy — "My brother glued my hand to the paper!"

Teacher — "How are you getting on with your science project, Freddy?"
Freddy — "It's inspiring, sir!"

Bill — "My brother gave me chickenpox!
  — He said it was better to give than to receive!"

How do you keep Mr Dopey busy?
Give him a piece of paper with P.T.O. written on both sides!

Fred — "I can read you like a book!"
Ted — "Oh? Do I have a happy ending?"

What do you do when a raging elephant steps on your foot?
Wait quietly until it steps off again!

What time is it when an elephant stands on your foot?
Time to call the doctor!

Teacher — "Inspiring?"

Freddy — "Yes sir, it's inspiring me to forget all about it and go out and play football!"

Teacher — "Did anyone see who wrote this rude word on the blackboard?"

Dim Tim — "I hope not, miss, or I'll be in big trouble!"

Teacher — "Tommy, how do you spell your name backwards?"

Tommy — "e-m-a-n-r-u-o-y!"

Teacher — "Now, can anyone find the lowest common denominator in this problem?"

Pupil — "Have you still not found that pesky thing?"

What is the difference between a doormat and a bottle of medicine?

One is taken up and shaken and the other is shaken up and taken!

Teacher — "What's 4+4, Katie?"

Katie — "8, Miss"

Teacher — "Good!"

Katie — "Good? It's perfect!"

Teacher — "Do you have a pet, Jimmy?"

Jimmy — "Yes, miss. I keep him in the pond and I call him Tiny."

Teacher — "Tiny? Why do you call him that?"

Jimmy — "Because he's my newt!"

Teacher — "Come on Tommy, it's not a difficult sum — a five year-old could do it!"
Tommy — "But I'm nine!"

Teacher — "Bobby, you haven't answered any of the questions in this maths test!"
Pupil — "I know, miss I wanted to be able to go home and tell my parents that I got nothing wrong!"

Teacher — "Why are you picking your nose in class, Jimmy?"
Jimmy — "Because I'm not allowed to do it at home!"
Teacher — "Billy, can you count to ten?"
Billy — "One two, three four, five, six, seven, eight, nine, ten."
Teacher — "Well done! Can you go on from there?"
Billy — "Jack, Queen, King, Ace!"

Teacher — "Annie, can you count from one to five?"
Annie — "One, two, three, four, five!"
Teacher — "Any higher?"
Annie (stands on chair) "One two, three, four, five!"

Bill — "I hear Lee won the Chinese cookery competition"
Will — "Yes, in fact you could say it was a wok-over!"

Fred — "I've signed up for Chinese cookery classes."
Ted — "Chinese cookery? That sounds difficult!"
Fred — "Not really, as long as you use your noodle."

Bill — "I could never eat goat meat!"
Will — "Why not?"
Bill — "Because my mother always said that butter wouldn't melt in my mouth!"

Where were lemons first found?
In a lemon tree!

What can a whole orange do that half an orange can't do?
Look round!

How do people eat cheese in Wales?
Caerphilly!

What kind of vegetables do drummers like best?
Beets!

Will — "I've invented a truth drink — would you like a taste?"
Bill — "Ugh! That tastes terrible!"
Will — "Ain't that the truth!"

How do you put your hair in a bun?
Stick your nose in a beefburger!

What's the difference between chili and chilli?
One 'l' of a difference!
What is small, green and hangs around?
A drip-dry gooseberry!

A sausage is lying on the refrigerator shelf, next to a fillet of salmon. The sausage tries to strike up a conversation with the fillet, but the fillet says nothing. After several minutes, chatting to the salmon fillet and getting no response, the sausage turns to the butter on his other side.

"See him over there?" he says, "He's a bit of a cold fish, isn't he?"

What did the fish-finger say to the tomato?
"That's enough of your sauce!

What cheese is made back to front?
Edam!

What kind of fruit begins with the letter 'N'?
'Nana!

What's green and full of bounce?
Spring cabbage!

What did one potato say to the other potato?
"This is a fine mash you've got us into!"

When is cheese like a nose with a cold?
When it's blue, smells and is runny!

How can you tell a dishonest sandwich?
It's full of baloney!

Why was the lemonade bottle crying?
It had lost its pop!

How do you please a piece of toast?
Butter it up a bit!

When is the pantry generous?
When it has a treat in store for you!

Why did the coffee mug crack?
The spoon made it stir-crazy!

Why did the strawberry call for help?
It was in a jam!

Why did the cucumber call for help?
It got into a pickle!

Why did no-one love the shrimp?
Because he was shellfish!

What kind of food do furniture-makers like best?
Veggie-tables!

What has no beginning, no end, and nothing in the middle?
A doughnut!

What is the most expensive food in the world?
The fortune cookie!

When is an apple pie like a headmaster?
When it's crusty and old!

What do card-players like to eat?
Ginger snaps!

What do choristers eat?
Hum-burgers and doh-nuts!

Which kind of meringues always come back?
Boo-meringues!

Turkey — "Brr — December's such a cold month, isn't it? I could do with something warm over me!"
Farmer — "How about some gravy?"

Why are Wimbledon players difficult customers in a restaurant?
Because whatever is served, it's sure to be returned!

What does Superman like to eat?
A hero sandwich!

What wobbles and flies?
A jellycopter!

What did the goalkeeper have for lunch?
Beans on post!

What kind of food is never ready for dinner parties?
Mayonnaise — it's always dressing!

What do gymnasts have for breakfast?
A few rolls!

What do bus drivers eat?
Cheap fare!

How do you stop fish from smelling?
Cut their noses off!

What lies under a tree with its tongue hanging out, covered in mustard?
A hot dog!

Why did the orange stop rolling downhill?
It ran out of juice!

What is green, edible and makes holes in trees?
Woody Woodpickle!

Why was the fruit shop assistant confused?
Because his boss told him to arrange the apples in pairs!

Two turkeys are sitting in the butcher's shop.
1st Turkey — "I'm never going to listen to another human being again!"
2nd Turkey — "Why not?"
1st Turkey — "The farmer said 'Trust me!' — then he trussed ME!"

Why do the strawberries go out in couples?
They don't like playing gooseberry!

Why is a sofa like a roast chicken?
They're both full of stuffing!

What is a doughnut?
A mad millionaire!

What two things can you never have for breakfast?
Lunch and dinner!

Why could the apple not get through to the orange on the telephone?
Because the lime was engaged!

Why are apples cheeky?
Because they give us plenty of sauce!

What did the orange say to its friend as they sat by the juice extractor?
"Squeezed to see you!"

What kind of fish is illegal?
Poached salmon!

What do karate experts like to eat best?
Chops!

What do lady race-drivers like to eat?
Pasta!

What do hippies like to eat?
Peas, man!

Who was the most popular artist in the police force?
Constable!

What do shoemakers like to eat?
Sole!

What do policemen have in their sandwiches?
Truncheon meat!

Sergeant — "Who's been using my notebook?"
Police officer — "Must have been PC Simpkins, Sarge. I'd know his prints anywhere!"
Sergeant — "Fingerprints?"
Police officer — "No, misprints! His spelling's terrible!"

What do reporters have in their sandwiches?
Front-page spread!

What do road menders like to eat?
Chips!

What did the policeman say to his stomach?
"You're under a vest!"

Newspaper headline — Mystery thief steals lightbulbs from police station. Police are still in the dark.

Newspaper headline — Dog food stolen from pet shop. Police are looking for a man with strong teeth and a healthy coat.

Newspaper headline — River floods Police station. Police officers rescued by Tosh Smith, in Mack Black's boat. Police say Mack and Tosh kept them dry.

Newspaper headline — Model's arm washed up on beach. Police say this one's a bit of a poser.

News headline — Army drill sergeant goes missing. Police say they're giving it swift attentions.

Newspaper headline — Missing dogs —
Police say they are following a number of leads.

Newsflash — Rhubarb thefts — Police say suspects are in custardy!

News headline — Five campers charged with loitering within tent!

News headline — Dog has nine pups —
Police have charged her with littering!

Newspaper headline — Thefts from underwear store. Police in-vest-igating.

News headline — Planks stolen from builder's yard. Police hope to nail the culprit.

Newspaper headline — Theft from babywear shop
— Police have found the bootee!

Newsflash — Fireworks thefts — suspect banged up!

Newsflash — Sheepdog trials — sheepdogs plead not guilty!

Newsflash — Phantom wig thief — Police say they have him locked up!

Newsflash — Javelins stolen from stadium — Inspector spearheads enquiry.

Newsflash — Dogfood thefts — Police say they've collared a suspect.

Newspaper headline — Missing crosswords — Police looking for clues.

Newspaper headline — China Thefts — Police studying mugshots.

Newsflash — Man has all holiday clothes stolen — Police are looking into the case.

Newspaper headline — Shirt thief — Police have got him in cuffs.

Newspaper headline — Broken window mystery — Police have cracked it!

Newspaper headline — Constable steals hair bleach — Police say it's a fair cop!

Newspaper headline — Demolition man charged with home-icide!

Newspaper headline — Holiday snaps stolen — Police have identified prints.

Newspaper headline — Theft of gold paint and balloons — Police have found gilty party.

Newspaper headline — Police station gets new lawn — Criminals say who grassed?

Newspaper headline — Holes appear in garden of MI6 building. Police suspect a mole.

Newspaper headline — Policeman learning semaphore causes havoc at road junction.

Newspaper headline — Earth tremor hits police headquarters. Police are shaken.

Newspaper headline — Government secrets sold to enemy agents by man in violet suit. Police are looking for the purpletraitor.

Newsflash — Thefts from Municipal Dump — Police have received a tip-off.

Newsflash — Stable hand murdered — Police are making horse-to-horse enquiries.

Newsflash — Cat found dead in mysterious circumstances — Police are making mouse-to-mouse enquiries.

Newsflash — Bo Peep's sheep taken — police have arrested crook!

Newspaper headline — Ten tons of soap missing from factory. Police say burglars made a clean getaway.

Newsflash — Two hundred blankets stolen from hotel. Police say there's been a cover-up.

Newsflash — Pig farm robbery. Perpetrators caught. Crooks ask 'Who squealed?'

Newsflash — 100 pairs of curling tongs stolen from factory. Police say it's a crime wave.

PC Plod — "I'm off on the beat now, sergeant."
Sergeant — "And may the force be with you!"

Criminal — "How did you know I was lying?"
Police officer — "Easy — your lips moved!"

Police officer — "And how did the intruder get in?"
Home owner — "Intruder window, of course!"

Did you hear about the police officer who caught a
falling star?
He charged it with glittering!

Sergeant — "And does the suspect have a record?"
Police officer — "No, sergeant, but he has quite a large CD
collection!"

Police officer — "I'm afraid your son has been run over
by a steamroller, Mrs Bloggs!"
Mrs Bloggs — "How is he feeling?
Police Officer — "Rather flat!"

Police officer — "I'm afraid your husband has been run
over by a steamroller, Mrs Smith!"
Mrs Smith — "Slide him into an envelope and send him
home!"

Police officer — "I've had reports that your son has been
throwing stones at the next door neighbour, Mr Jones!"
Mr Jones — "No need to worry, officer, he's got a rotten
aim!"

Car driver — "Excuse me, officer, but can you tell me if my indicator light is working?"
Police officer — "It is — it isn't — it is — it isn't — it is..."

What do policemen in Hawaii say when they see someone acting suspiciously?
"Alo-ha, alo-ha, alo-ha, what have we got here, then?"!

Policeman (to driver of crashed vehicle) — "Now then, can you tell me what happened?"
Driver — "No, officer, I can't — my eyes were shut at the time!"

Why do police cars have radios?
So that the officers don't have to listen to each other!

Man — "How do you know it was my car that knocked over the lamppost, officer?"
PC Plod — "I found the 'eavy dents on your vehicle, sir!"

What did the policeman say when he cut himself shaving?
"I'm nicked!"

Newsflash — Burglary in lingerie store — Police say robbers gave them the slip.

Policeman — "I'm putting you in the cells for the night, mate!"
Criminal — "What's the charge?"
Policeman — "No charge — it's absolutely free!"

Criminal — "I've spent four years making the Queen happy!"
Friend — "What do you mean?"
Criminal — "I've been serving her Majesty's pleasure!"

Former prisoner — "I could see the lock of the cell door was easy to pick, so I put my little finger in the keyhole and twisted. . ."
Friend — "And then?"
Former prisoner — "I broke my fingernail!"

Newsflash — Lorry with load of strawberries and sugar has overturned on the motorway. Police are dealing with the jam.

Why was the police officer not allowed to search the rabbit hole?
Because he didn't have a warren-t!

PC Bloggs waved down a car one day, because the driver was continually sounding the horn.
"As keeper of the peace, I order your peeper to cease!" he said.

Notice on toy-shop window "Bicycle horns for sale. Come in and take a peep!"

Notice on roofing contractor's office door "Gone for lunch. Slater!"

Notice on Italian restaurant's door "Closed. It's pasta our bedtime!"

Notice on computer shop window "Back in five minutes. Gone for chips!"

Notice on plumber's window "Doorbell not working. Tap on door."

Notice on baker's shop window. "Taking a nap. Doughnut disturb."

Notice on fridge door from maths teacher to his wife "Add sums for lunch. Do you minus having take-away for supper?"

Notice on lawyer's office door "Gone for lunch. Back suin'!"

Notice on beautician's window "Unsightly blemishes? On-the spot-treatment available!"

Notice on hairdresser's window "Sorry, we're closed. Comb back tomorrow!"

Notice on barber's window "Closed. Urgent appointment elsewhere. Moustache!"

Notice on chip-shop window "Closed for holidays. Open again next Fry day!"

Knock-knock!
Who's there?
Sacha!
Sacha who?
Sacha lot of questions! Just let me in, will you!

Knock-knock!
Who's there?
Buster!
Buster who?
Buster London, broken down outside in the street!

Knock-knock!
Who's there?
Barbara!
Barbara who?
Barbara Black Sheep!

Knock-knock!
Who's there?
Europe!
Europe who?
Europe early today!

Knock-knock!
Who's there?
Arthur!
Arthur who?
Arthur got what I came for!

Knock-knock!
Who's there?
Toby!
Toby who?
Toby or not Toby, that is the question. . ."

What the daddy rabbit tell his friends when his wife had more babies?
"Fresh buns today!"

1st boy — "I don't feel very well — I've got butterflies in my stomach!"
2nd boy — "Huh! You're lucky! I've got a school dinner in mine!

Billy — "I can't wind my watch!"
Bob — "Why not?"
Billy — "I lost it a week ago!"

Knock-knock!
Who's there?
Ida!
Ida who
Ida feeling I might find you here!

Knock-knock!
Who's there?
Jamaica!
Jamaica who?
Jamaica habit of leaving your visitors standing out here
in the cold like this?

Knock-knock!
Who's there?
Rupert!
Rupert who?
Rupert your left leg in, your left leg out. . ."

Knock-knock!
Who's there?
Martin!
Martini who?
Martini hand is frozen!

Notice on door of nuclear power station "Gone fission!"

Knock-knock!
Who's there?
Owl!
Owl who?
Owl you know unless you open the door?

Knock-knock!
Who's there?
Watt!
Watt who?
Watt the Dickens are you doing in my house?

Knock-knock!
Who's there?
Sibelius!
Sibelius who?
Sibelius broken again!

Knock-knock!
Who's there?
Juno!
Juno who?
Juno my name? I've forgotten!

Knock-knock!
Who's there?
Alice!
Alice who?
Alice-ened at the door, so I knew you were in!

Newsflash — Singing burglars — Police continue with enchoiries.

Knock-knock!
Who's there?
Red!
Red who?
Red the sign that says your doorbell's broken!

Knock-knock!
Who's there?
Lena
Lena who?
Lena little closer to the door and see if you can recognise my voice!

Knock-knock!
Who's there?
Ammonia!
Ammonia who?
Ammonia little boy, and I can't reach the handle!

Knock-knock!
Who's there?
Sindy!
Sindy who?
Sindy payment for your new doorknocker to my house!

Knock-knock!
Who's there?
Few!
Few who?
Few were me you wouldn't be happy being left out here in the cold!

Knock-knock!
Who's there?
M. Brown!
M. Brown who?
M. Brown and fit after my foreign holiday!

Knock-knock!
Who's there?
Jupiter!
Jupiter who?
Jupiter hurry or you'll be late for your meeting!

Knock-knock!
Who's there?
Phil!
Phil who?
Philthy weather out here — open the door!

Knock-knock!
Who's there?
Candy!
Candy who?
Candy owner of the red car outside please move it?

Knock-knock!
Who's there?
Mima!
Mima who?
Mima fingers! They're shut in the door!

Knock-knock!
Who's there?
Lefty!
Lefty who?
Lefty iron on — gotta go back home!

The edition published 2008 by
Geddes & Grosset,
David Dale House,
New Lanark, ML11 9DJ, Scotland

© 2008 Geddes & Grosset

ISBN 978 1 84205 673 8

Printed and bound in the UK